Hayner Family History

From Weinheim, Kurpfalz, Germany to Madison, West Virginia, U.S.A.

I0116139

Hayner

Melinda Clayton

Hayner Family History:

From Weinheim, Kurpfalz, Germany
to Madison, West Virginia, U.S.A.

Copyright © 2020 Melinda Clayton

Published by Thomas-Jacob Publishing, LLC
TJPub@thomas-jacobpublishing.com

Title font: Black Chancery. Public domain font created by Doug Miles and Earl Allen in 1993. Available online from 1001fonts.com.

Library of Congress Control Number: 2020903416
1. Reference/Genealogy and Heraldry 2. Family and Relationships/Reference
ISBN-10: 1-950750-30-2
ISBN-13: 978-1-950750-30-6
Thomas-Jacob Publishing, LLC, Deltona, Florida

First Edition
First Printing: 2020
Printed in the United States of America

For my mother

Table of Contents

Author's Note

In 2018, when I worked with my father to research the family history of his side of my family (*Franklin Family History: From 1425 England to 2018 U.S.A.*, by William M. Franklin), we began by explaining the method we chose to use for our research.

As we explained then, it can be difficult to know which path to follow, particularly when family history spans hundreds of years and two different continents. The matter is made even more complicated due to the fact that historically, women have taken on the surname of their husbands.

As we explained back then, for these reasons, and to streamline the process as much as possible, I followed the surname Hayner, beginning with my grandfather, from son to father all the way back to Leonhart Hüner, who died in

Weinheim, Germany around 1597 (Hensell, 1958).

The name Hayner has been spelled many different ways through the generations; Hüner, Heiner, Hiner, Haner, Haynor, and Hayner are just a few of the variations. My mother remembers relatives in her part of West Virginia who spelled their name differently from the way her family of origin spelled theirs. As I proceed through our specific family line, I'll use the spelling most often used through the various sources consulted.

To further complicate matters, the same family names are used repeatedly throughout the generations, which has at times caused confusion for those working to put together a family history. In those instances, I'll discuss both the areas of confusion and also my rationale for moving forward as I have.

It's worth noting that throughout the generations the Hayner men often married more than once, choosing a second wife and beginning a new family after the first wife died. For the purposes of this book, I've only included the wives who are the mothers of our direct ancestors. It's also worth noting that the number of first wives and infants and children who died over the generations is both striking and sobering.

The information here is as accurate as I'm able to make it. A bibliography of sources used can be found in the back of the book.

Introduction

*I*t would be impossible to discuss the history of my particular branch of the Hayner family without including a brief discussion of the Thirty Years War.

One of the longest-lasting wars in history, the Thirty Years War ultimately killed over eight million people across Europe, either from the battles themselves, or from the resulting disease, poverty, and famine (History.com Editors, 2020).

Lasting from 1618 to 1648, the Thirty Years War began as a battle between Catholics and Protestants but eventually evolved into a battle over the control of much of Europe. As a result, it changed history in many ways, from redrawing the geopolitical face of Europe, to decimating families and wiping out genealogical records.

Such was the case with my specific branch of the Hayner family. As Hensell (1958) noted, the Thirty Years War wiped out most records from Weinheim, Germany such that the oldest ancestor we can find is Leonhart Hüner, date of birth unknown, date of death estimated to be sometime around 1597.

The Hüner Family: Weinheim, Germany

It's always fascinating to learn what one's ancestors did hundreds of years ago, and the Hayner family is no exception. As it turns out, the Hüners of Weinheim, Germany, were barber-surgeons (Hensell, 1958).

I must admit, until undertaking this research, I'd never heard of barber-surgeons, but as Pelling (2013) explains, in medieval Europe, barbers were considered medical practitioners who actually performed surgery. They often had no formal training, and in some cases were illiterate; however, their skills were sorely needed, particularly in times of war.

In keeping with the history of the profession, the red and white barber poles of today have a bit of a sordid history. The red was historically understood to signify the blood lost during procedures such as bloodletting, amputations, treating wounds, and setting bones. The

7

white was understood to represent the bandages used to stem the flow of blood for each procedure (Nix, 2018).

According to Pelling (2013) the financial status of barber-surgeons varied greatly. Although we don't have specific information regarding Leonhart's financial and social status, we do know he was a land owner. Hensell (1958) includes information from court documents indicating that after Leonhart's death, his widow was involved in several transactions in which she sold land, including portions of vineyards.

We don't know where Leonhart Hüner was born, but Hensell (1958) speculates it may have been "the Duchy of Junich, or the lower Rhine country" (p. 8). According to Hensell (1958) he died in Weinheim, Kurpfalz, Germany around the year 1597. We know that he was married to Agatha Schneider, and that they had at least one son: Herman Huner, 1590-1654.

Dates of birth and death in this section were provided by Hensell (1958) unless otherwise noted.

———————————

Herman Huner (1590-1654), son of Leonhart and Agatha, is also described by Hensell (1958) as a "citizen and physician (or barber) of Weinheim (p. 9). Herman married Magdalena Leist,

and they had at least one son: Hans Bartel
Huner, 1628-1682.

Hans Bartel Huner (1628-1682), son of Herman
and Magdalena, is also described by Hensell
(1958) as a citizen and physician. Hans Bartel
married Apollonia Muller and they had the following children:

  1. Hans Adam Huner was born on February 24, 1662 and died on November 8,
  1702. We are direct descendants of
  Hans Adam Huner.

  2. Herman Huner 1664-1668

  3. Barbra Huner 1666-1674

  4. Anna Huner 1669-1674

  5. Herman Huner 1672-unknown

  6. Hans Peter Huner 1677-1681

Hans Adam Huner (1662-1702), son of Hans
Bartel and Apollonia, was also a citizen and physician. He married Rosina Ortliep, and they had
the following children:

  1. Hans Philipp Huner 1685-1731

2. Johannas Huner, 1689-unknown

3. Hans Adam Huner 1690-unknown

4. Philipp Jacob Huner was born on April 30, 1693. His date of death is unknown. We are direct descendants of Philipp Jacob Humer.

5. Anna Marie Huner, 1697-unknown

———————————

Philipp Jacob Huner (1693-unknown), son of Hans Adam and Rosina, married, but the name of his wife is unknown. Some online genealogy sites list her as Gertant, but I have not been able to find a source for this. According to Hensell (1958), Philipp Jacob had one son: Philip Huner, born in 1718, date of death unknown.

Philip Huner, son of Philipp Jacob Huner, immigrated to America in 1738.

The Hayner Family Arrives in America

$\mathcal{M}$any public family trees on Ancestry.com have Philip Huner's (1718-unknown) middle name as Eamer, but Hensell (1958) does not include a middle name, and my research indicates Eamer may have been a middle name given to future generations.

Hensell (1958) also doesn't include any information about Philip's wife, but some online genealogy sites list her as Mary Magdalene Berner (or Burner) born in 1730. This is questionable, however, because if that birth year is accurate, some of Philip's children listed by Hensell (1958) would have been born before Mary Magdalene Berner was of childbearing age.

Other online genealogy sites list Philip's wife as Catrina Luserin, born in 1725. Although I'm unable to find a source validating the name of either woman, it's certainly possible Philip married twice, as did many of our male ancestors along the line.

What we do know is that Philip arrived in Pennsylvania in 1738 at the age of 20. The name of the ship was *Nancy*, and the captain was William Wallace. Philip took the "oath of allegiance" on September 20, 1738 (Hensell, 1958). Moving forward, the last name of Philip's children is listed by Hensell (1958) as Heiner.

Philip (1718-unknown) had the following children:

1. John Heiner, dates of birth and death unknown, served in the Revolutionary War (Hensell, 1958).

2. Emanual Heiner, dates of birth and death unknown.

3. Joseph Heiner 1739-unknown

4. Jacob Heiner 1742-unknown

5. Elizabeth Heiner 1745-unknown

6. Henry Heiner 1749-1826, served in the Revolutionary War (Hensell, 1958).

7. Frederick Heiner 1752-unknown, served in the Revolutionary War (Hensell, 1958).

8. Johann Ludwig Heiner was born on July 14, 1754, and died on June 6, 1828

(Ancestry.com. *U.S., Find A Grave Index, 1600s-Current*). Hensell (1958) omits the first name of Johann, instead referring to him as Ludwig/Louis Heiner, but Johann Ludwig Heiner is the name used in both military and burial records.

Hensell (1958) also omits Johann Ludwig's military record, but Private Johann Ludwig Heiner fought in the Revolutionary War along with his brothers under the command of a Captain Haeffer (Ancestry.com *Pennsylvania, Veterans Burial Cards, 1777-2012*). Although records for Johann Ludwig are sparse, my sources indicate we are his direct descendants.

To help alleviate confusion, from this point forward I'll refer to this man as Johann Ludwig/Lewis.

And this is where internet sources and print sources become both confused and confusing.

Johann Ludwig Louis/Lewis Heiner/ Haner

*H*ensell (1958) leaves us here, veering off to explore Frederick and his descendants, his own family's branch. A handful of public family trees online attempt to connect our particular branch to Frederick as well, but my sources indicate we're actually descended from Johann Ludwig/Lewis, son of Philip and brother of Frederick, a man who proved very difficult to track down.

A handful of the public family trees I stumbled across online listed both a Lewis (or Louis) and a Johann Ludwig as sons of Philip and brothers of Frederick, but the trees that did offered no follow-up information on Lewis/Louis, and the online records linked for Lewis/Louis actually took me to sources for Johann Ludwig. During my research for various projects I often come across family trees that list the same family member multiple times under different spellings of the name. In this case, unless further information comes to light, I'll continue to use Hensell's (1958) list of Philip's children as my source.

In addition to the issue of differently spelled names, records linked to by participants on online genealogy sites sometimes don't match specific aspects of an ancestor's life experiences. For example, records linked in order to support residency for a specific ancestor may contain the name of that relative, but the dates of birth and/or death don't align with that specific individual. Because some of the online sites allow users to automatically populate their own family trees using information from other public family trees, errors are repeated not only across trees, but across sites.

Many times, I've followed the trail to a linked census report, record of marriage, etc., only to realize the name is right, but the year listed is well before the birth or after the death of the specific ancestor for whom I'm searching. When I dig more deeply, I sometimes discover the record linked to is a different ancestor or descendant. In other cases, aside from the name, there appears to be no connection between that person and my family at all—at least, not on this side of the ocean.

My method when researching family history is to take hints provided on online genealogy sites and find sourced information to back up the claims made.

As mentioned earlier, when I first began researching my mother's family, I came across a few public family trees that attempted to connect our line to Frederick, son of Philip, our immigrant to North America. This doesn't work for several reasons, first and foremost because Hensell (1958), who is directly descended from Frederick, provided extensive research into that branch of the family, and ancestors known to be in our direct line, such as my grandfather, great-grandfather, and great-great grandfather, are not a part of that line.

Furthermore, the names I saw most often linked as sons to Frederick, son of our immigrant Philip, were Lewis and Noah.

As discussed earlier, Frederick had a brother named Johann Ludwig/Lewis, and he also had a great-nephew named Lewis (and no doubt many other relatives named Ludwig/Louis/Lewis whose threads I haven't followed), but he did not have a son named Lewis.

Noah, a direct ancestor on our branch whom we'll learn more about later, was actually the son of a *different* Frederick Haner. *That* Frederick Haner was the son of a man called Lewis

Haner who showed up in Kanawha County, Virginia around 1806 (Hayner et al., 2001). I believe that man was actually Johann Ludwig Heiner, son of immigrant Philip and brother to Frederick.

That belief is based, in part, on the information below:

- We know that the children of immigrant Philip Heiner, including Frederick (b. 1752) and Johann Ludwig (b. 1754), were born in York County, Pennsylvania in Paradise Township, a tiny community on the outskirts of Abbottstown (Hensell, 1958).

- We know from Hensell (1958) that Philip's sons John, Henry, and Frederick fought in the Revolutionary War. Although Hensell (1958) does not include Ludwig in his list of war veterans, we know that Johann Ludwig Heiner also fought in the Revolutionary War under the command of a Captain Haeffer (Ancestry.com *Pennsylvania, Veterans Burial Cards, 1777-2012*). This matches what my family's oral history has always stated to be true: that we have a direct ancestor who fought alongside several brothers in the Revolutionary War.

- We know that our particular branch of the Hayner family showed up in the Big

Creek area of what was at that time Kanawha County, Virginia (now Logan County, West Virginia) after the Revolutionary War and around the early 1800s (Hayner et al., 2001; Ragland & Dorsey, 1978).

• We know from Ragland and Dorsey (1978) that Frederick Haner (notice the spelling of the surname at this point), a "hero of the Revolution," settled "at a very early date at the mouth of Big Creek" (Chapter XV).

• We know that Johann Ludwig eventually incorporated Louis (Hensell, 1958), or Lewis, into his name.

• Hayner et al. (2001) tell us that Lewis Haner, surname spelled the same as Frederick's, came to the Big Creek area around 1806, settling with his wife and five children.

This differs from what Hensell (1958) tells us. In addition to omitting his first name and military service, Hensell (1958) writes that although Johann Ludwig married a woman named Barbra Fegeli, he had no known children.

To add to the confusion, a couple of online genealogy sites I browsed listed one child, a son named Henrich, but the birthdate listed for Henrich was earlier than the birthdates of both Johann Ludwig and Barbra, so that's clearly not possible. Those family trees also listed one of Henrich Heiner's sons as Johann Ludwig, an indication that there may be a Johann Ludwig/Henrich connection somewhere, but it doesn't appear to be in our direct line.

On this topic, given that Hensell (1958) overlooked other important details about Johann Ludwig (Hensell's person of interest was Frederick, after all), Hayner et al. (2001) seem to have the most reliable information. They tell us Lewis Haner was born between 1750 and 1760 (we know from previously cited sources that Johann Ludwig was born in 1754), and that "[T]his gentleman farmer was the earliest known progenitor of the Haner-Hayner-Haynor-Hainor clan of Logan and Boone Counties. ... Lewis Haner came with his wife, whose name is unknown, and children to establish a domicile on the Trace Fork of Big Creek" (p. 265).

• *Sims Index to Land Grants in West Virginia* (Sims, 2003) lists a Lewis Haner as having bought 50 acres on Big Creek in 1814.

- Hayner et al. (2001) also tell us Lewis Haner eventually left Big Creek in favor of Ohio; however, my research does not support a move to Ohio for this particular Lewis. What I did find, through Ancestry.com. *1870 United States Federal Census*, is that a Lewis Hayner born in 1815 married a Nancy Smith and at some point left Kanawha County, Virginia for Guyan Township, Ohio, but this was actually the grandson of the Lewis under discussion (Hayner et al., 2001).

- That's not to say that this particular Lewis Haner did not leave Big Creek. According to Hensell (1958), Ludwig/Louis Heiner was buried in Abbottstown, PA, just outside the tiny town in which he was born, on an unknown date. According to Ancestry.com. *Pennsylvania, Veterans Burial Cards, 1777-2012*, Johann Ludwig Heiner was buried in Abbottstown, PA on June 6, 1828.

Were Hensell's (1958) Johann Ludwig/Louis Heiner and Hayner et al.'s (2001) Lewis Haner one and the same? I believe they were, not only based on the information above, but also on additional information we'll discuss moving forward.

By the time Frederick Haner, son of immigrant Philip, appeared in Kanawha County, Virginia, the spelling of the last name had become Haner according to Ragland and Dorsey (1978).

The list of children born to Lewis Haner, provided by Hayner et al. (2001), indicates their last name was also now spelled Haner:

1. James Haner, dates of birth and death unknown. *Sims Index to Land Grants in WV* (Sims, 2003) shows a James Haner as having bought a total of 200 acres on Big Creek in 1814.

2. Jacob Haner 1783-unknown. *Sims Index to Land Grants in WV* (Sims, 2003) shows a Jacob Haner as having purchased a total of 90 acres along Big Creek in 1814.

3. Frederick Haner was born in 1785, and his date of death is unknown. *Sims Index to Land Grants in WV* (Sims, 2003) shows a Frederick Haner as having purchased a total of 50 acres along Big Creek in 1825. We are the direct descendants of Frederick Haner.

4. William Haner, dates of birth and death unknown. Hayner et al. (2001) state that other than one mention in local documents, no other mention of William can be found.

5. Unnamed daughter, listed in the 1890 census, but dates of birth and death unknown (Hayner et al., 2001).

———————————

Frederick Haner (1785-1873), son of Johann Ludwig/Lewis, was born in Pennsylvania but listed in the 1820 census of Cabell County, Virginia (Ancestry.com. *1820 United States Federal Census)* and in the 1850 census of Boone County, Virginia (Hayner et al., 2001). According to Hayner et al. (2001), he married Frances S. Barker and had the following children:

1. Elizabeth "Libby" Haner 1812-1857

2. Lewis Haner 1813-unknown

3. Francis Haner 1814-1870

4. Noah Haner was born on February 4, 1815 and died on May 17, 1855 in Logan County, Virginia (now West Virginia). We are the direct descendants of Noah Haner.

5. Sarah Sally Haner 1817-1880

6. Nancy Haner 1818-1889

This is another area in which both online and print sources indicate some confusion, specifically in regard to Noah. What's not disputed is that he lived; what is disputed is who, exactly, he came from.

When all the threads are untangled, it is this dispute that provides the most compelling evidence that Hensell's (1958) Johann Ludwig/Louis Heiner is indeed Hayner et al.'s (2001) Lewis Haner of Big Creek.

Noah Haner

*A*s with the previous confusion regarding brothers Frederick and Johann Ludwig/Lewis, the confusion here seems to once again stem from an attempt to connect our specific line to the first Frederick, Johann Ludwig/Lewis' brother, instead of to Johann Ludwig/Lewis' son Frederick.

Case in point: Ragland and Dorsey (1978) state that Frederick was a "hero of the Revolution" (Ch. XV) who settled early along Big Creek in Logan County. He also states (erroneously) that Frederick had only one son, James, who died young without children. Ragland and Dorsey (1978) then state (also erroneously) that Frederick had three daughters: a) Nancy, who married George Fry, b) Frances, who married Obadiah Godby, and c) Polly, who remained unmarried but gave birth to four children, one of whom was Noah.

According to my research, there are several errors in this passage. We'll begin with the fact that the Frederick that Ragland and Dorsey (1978) reference is clearly Johann Ludwig/Lewis' brother and not his son. Johann Ludwig/Lewis' brother Frederick (b. 1752), son of our immigrant Philip, fought in the Revolutionary war, but Johann Ludwig/Lewis' son Frederick wasn't born until 1785 (Hayner et al., 2001).

While it's Johann Ludwig/Lewis' brother Frederick that Ragland and Dorsey (1978) are referencing, the children they reference belonged to Johann Ludwig/Lewis' *son* Frederick.

Johann Ludwig/Lewis' *brother* Frederick's children, who were thoroughly researched by Hensell (1958), were Robert, John, Elizabeth, and Sussana.

Remember from our previous list that the children of Johann Ludwig/Lewis' *son* Frederick included Nancy (b. 1818), who married George Fry, and Francis (b. 1814), who married Obadiah Godby (Hayner et al., 2001). They do not, however, include an unmarried daughter named Polly who gave birth to a son named Noah. Instead they include Frederick's own son named Noah, brother to the aforementioned Nancy and Francis (and Elizabeth, Lewis, and Sarah).

Furthermore, the grandchildren of Johann Ludwig/Lewis and children of Frederick were all born between 1812-1818 (Hayner et al., 2001). Noah's birth year is listed in multiple places as 1815, falling in line nicely with his siblings.

To summarize, two of the children (Nancy and Frances) listed by Ragland and Dorsey (1978) as belonging to Frederick Haner, Revolutionary War hero and son of our immigrant Philip, were actually the children of Frederick Haner, son of Lewis Haner of Big Creek.

But what about Ragland and Dorsey's (1978) assertion that Frederick, Revolutionary War hero and son of our immigrant Philip, had a deceased son named James? And what about an unwed daughter named Polly?

It was actually Lewis Haner of Big Creek who had a son named James who died childless, leaving behind a wife named Mary "Polly" Stallings Haner (Hayner et al., 2001).

This accidental mixing and mingling of the children and grandchildren of Frederick, Revolutionary War hero and son of our immigrant Philip, and Lewis Haner of Big Creek further serves to demonstrate that Hensell's (1958) Johann Ludwig/Louis, son of our immigrant Philip, and Hayner et al.'s (2001) Lewis Haner of Big Creek were one and the same.

In the end, we'll probably never know how the threads became so tangled. What we do know, however, is that we are descended from

Noah, and that he appears to be the first from our line who was both born and buried in what was at that time the Big Creek area of Virginia (now Logan County, West Virginia).

The Hayners in West Virginia

Noah Haner (1815-1855) married Mary Elizabeth Barker (Ragland & Dorsey, 1978). According to Hayner et al. (2001), they had the following children:

1. Emily 1835-unknown

2. Letha J. 1840-unknown

3. Susannah 1843-unknown

4. Nancy Ann 1844-unknown

5. William A. Haner was born April 30, 1847 and died February 22, 1903. We are direct descendants of William A. Haner.

6. John Simms 1849-unknown

7. Joseph Benjamin 1851-unknown

8. Lewis David 1853-unknown

William A. Haner (1847-1855) married Mary Clementine Stowers. According to Hayner et al. (2001), they had the following children:

1. John Marshall Haner was born on December 12, 1875, and died on February 17, 1947. We are direct descendants of John Marshall Haner.

2. William Elbert Haner 1877-unknown

3. Lena Mae Haner 1880-unknown

4. Linnie Maude Haner 1880-unknown (twin to Lena May)

5. Eliza Ann 1888-unknown

6. Stella Haner 1890-1891

7. Herbert Haner 1892-1908

John Marshall Hayner (1875-1947) was born in Logan County, West Virginia and fought in the Spanish American War. According to an application to U.S. Headstone Applications for Military Veterans, which was filed on December 12, 1950 by daughter Thelma Hayner Ferrell, John enlisted on June 25, 1898. A private in Company K, he received an honorable discharge April 10,

1899. Shortly after his discharge, he married Eliza Anne "Annie" Lilly on April 20, 1899 (Hayner et al., 2001), and they had the following children:

1. Wallace G. Hayner 1900-unknown

2. Willard Hayner 1902-unknown

3. Ray Hayner was born on August 21, 1904 and died on November 19, 1984. Ray Hayner was this writer's grandfather.

4. Mary Josephine Hayner Peyton 1906-1997

5. Thelma Hayner Ferrell 1909-1965

6. Floyd Leslie Hayner 1911-2006

7. Basil Hayner 1914-2001

8. Nina Murell Hayner Hargis 1916-1998

Although Hayner et al. (2001) state John changed the spelling of the name to Hayner, it remains Haner on both his death certificate and the application for a headstone. According to his death certificate, John's cause of death was prostate cancer. He died in Veterans Memorial Hospital in Huntington, West Virginia at 11:40 p.m. on February 17, 1947 and is buried in Peyton

Family Cemetery in Leet, West Virginia, a small unincorporated town located in Lincoln County.

Ray Hayner was born on August 21, 1904. His WWII Draft Registration Card lists Fayette County, West Virginia as his place of birth, but according to the United States Federal Census of 1910, by the age of six he was living in Chapmanville, West Virginia, which is located in Logan County.

By 1920 he was living in Harts Creek, West Virginia, in Lincoln County. (Of note: the census of 1920 lists his age at that time as 15, but we know from Social Security records that he was born in 1904 so would have been sixteen in 1920.)

The census of 1930 lists his residence as Big Ugly Creek Unimproved Dirt Road in Harts Creek, West Virginia. His occupation at that time is "Laborer," with the industry listed as "General Farm." Class of Worker is "Unpaid Worker, member of the family."

In his younger adulthood, Ray, a brother, and a cousin spent some time wandering the countryside, hopping trains and hitchhiking. When I asked my mother if they were traveling the country for pleasure or looking for work, she replied that it was probably a bit of both.

During the Depression, Ray worked a variety of jobs associated with the Works Progress Administration (WPA), including building and repairing roads and bridges, constructing buildings, and anything else that was offered.

Ray Hayner married Ruby Mabel Woodrum (June 15, 1909-August, 11, 1984) on January 22, 1933. The census of 1940 continues to list his residence as Harts Creek and also notes that he completed school in the 8th grade and that the house he and his wife and children were living in was rented.

It was around this time that Ray moved the family to Madison. According to my mother, he found work in a coal mine in Wharton, West Virginia that was owned by Pennsylvania Coal and Coke Company, and he remained there until he retired.

Ray and Ruby had the following children:

1. Connie June Hayner Miller 1934-

2. Faye Hayner Cole 1936-2017

3. Larry "Buster" Hayner 1936–

4. Norvel "Sam" Hayner 1939 – 2019

5. Patty Lynn Hayner Franklin was born on July 5, 1941. She is this writer's mother.

6. Carol Kay Hayner Hayden 1944-2018

7. Teresa Jo Hayner Waits 1956-2015. Teresa was actually the daughter of Faye, but was raised for most of her childhood by Ray and Ruby.

Ray Hayner died on November 19, 1984, just over two months after the death of his wife and my grandmother, Ruby Mabel Woodrum.

Final Notes

The Hayner name continues for our branch, of course, from the sons of Ray Hayner and their sons and grandsons.

My cataloging of the Hayner history stops here, however, for several reasons. Primary among those reasons is that the stories of the living descendants of Leonhart Hüner are not mine to tell.

What I can tell is that Patty Lynn Hayner met William M. Franklin while she was working in Washington D.C. after a stint as a student at Marshall University. William, who was in the U.S. Navy, was stationed in Maryland. Patty and William married on December 18, 1963 in Lexington Park, Maryland.

After William's navel service ended in March 1969, William and Patty, with two children at that time, moved to Covington, TN where William grew up. They built a home on one acre of the 25-acre farm his parents owned.

William and Patty had a total of five children, and they are as follows:

1. William Michael, born in 1965.

2. Melinda Rae, born in 1967.

3. Tracy Renee, born in 1972.

4. Samuel Joseph, born in 1980.

5. Amanda Susan, born in 1982.

After building their home on the family farm in 1970, Patty and William both completed college. Patty has a B.A. in English from Lambuth College. William M. has a B.A. in Religion from Lambuth College and an MDiv in Theology from Vanderbilt University.

Patty retired from teaching school in 1999, and William retired as a United Methodist Minister in 2005. They bought the remaining part of the 25-acre farm from family members after William's parents died, and this is where they continue to live.

Bibliography

Ancestry.com. *1820 United States Federal Census* [database on-line]. Provo, UT, USA: Ancestry.com Operations, Inc., 2010. Images reproduced by FamilySearch.

Ancestry.com. *1870 United States Federal Census* [database on-line]. Provo, UT, USA: Ancestry.com Operations, Inc., 2009. Images reproduced by FamilySearch.

Ancestry.com. *Pennsylvania, Veterans Burial Cards, 1777-2012* [database on-line]. Provo, UT, USA: Ancestry.com Operations, Inc., 2010.

Ancestry.com. *U.S., Find A Grave Index, 1600s-Current* [database on-line]. Provo, UT, USA: Ancestry.com Operations, Inc., 2012.

Hayner, J. A., Hayner, M. B., & Hayner, F. W. (2001). *History of the Hayner family: the descendants of Johannes Haner, 1710-1966.* Salem, MA: Higginson Book Co. Retrieved from http://haynerfamily.org/Home_Page.html

Hensell, J. (1958). *Chronicles of a Germany family, or, Heiners of Germany, Pennsylvania, Kentucky, and Texas.* Retrieved from https://hdl.hadle.net/2027/wu.89062877113

History.com Editors. (2020, February 9). *Thirty Years War*. History. https://www.history.com/topics/reformation/thirty-years-war

Nix, E. "Why Are Barber Poles Red, White and Blue?" *History.com*, A&E Television Networks. www.history.com/news/why-are-barber-poles-red-white-and-blue.

Pelling, M. (2013). *Common Lot: Sickness, Medical Occupations and the Urban Poor in Early Modern England*. Place of publication not identified: Routledge.

Ragland, H.C. & Dorsey, D. R. (1978). *History of Logan County, W. Va.: (genealogical section)*. Logan County Genealogical Society.

Sims, E. B. (2003). *Sims index to land grants in West Virginia*. Baltimore: Genealogical Pub. Co.

www.ingramcontent.com/pod-product-compliance
Lightning Source LLC
Chambersburg PA
CBHW060529280326
41933CB00014B/3118